THE BATSFORD COLOUR BOOK OF

Kent

Introduction and commentaries by
Judith Glover

B. T. BATSFORD LTD   LONDON

First published 1976
Text copyright Judith Glover 1976
Filmset by
Servis Filmsetting Ltd, Manchester
Printed and bound by
Lee-Fung Asco, Hong Kong
for the Publishers B. T. Batsford Ltd
4 Fitzhardinge Street, London W1H 0AH

ISBN 0 7134 3153 9

Contents

Acknowledgments

The Author and Publishers would like to thank the following for permission to reproduce the transparencies which appear in this book:

Peter Baker, page 45;
J. Allan Cash, page 61;
Noel Habgood, pages 23, 35, 37, 49;
A. F. Kersting, pages 17, 19, 21, 25, 27, 31, 33, 43, 53, 55;
Picturepoint, pages 29, 39;
Kenneth Scowen, pages 47, 51, 57, 59, 63;
Spectrum, page 41.

Introduction

'Kent, sir – everybody knows Kent – apples, cherries, hops, and women.'

Alfred Jingle was not a man given to understatement – quite the reverse – but for once his creator, Charles Dickens, permitted the strolling actor what a critic might justifiably have termed a masterpiece of underplaying. Kent has her apples, cherries, hops and women in abundance; but she has so much more besides. It is an instance of subject-associations and priorities, and Mr Jingle, talking, to use the modern term, 'off the top of his head', reveals something of himself through this brief and selective catalogue.

Mention Kent to anyone and request an instinctive reaction, and the result will vary to extremes. 'The Garden of England' is the handiest label; or 'the Gateway to England'; or 'the Little Kingdom'. All are true. England, for example, has many garden counties, but none fairer, more varied and productive than Kent. The seventeenth-century poet Michael Drayton summed it up neatly in *Polyolbion*:

> *What country hath this isle that can compare with thee,*
> *Which hast within thy self as much as thou canst wish?*
> *Thy conies, ven'son, fruit; thy sorts of fowl and fish:*
> *As what with strength comports, thy hay, thy corn, thy wood;*
> *Nor any thing doth want, that any where is good.*

Those apple orchards, whose springtime flowering brings convoys of cars and coaches to the county to take the staggeringly beautiful 'Blossom Route', were not once as trim and orderly as they are today. There have been apples in Kent since the first century AD, but it was not until the time of the Tudors that the first commercial orchard was planted, at Teynham. That best loved of all dessert apples, the Cox's Orange Pippin, was first cultivated in Kent, and she has many other varieties too, tens of thousands of square acres of them, making her

Britain's premier apple-growing county. As a bonus, the massed blossoms ensure the wellbeing of a vast bee population, and consequently some of the tastiest honey in the world.

The bees also feast well in the many cherry orchards – Kentish cherries, like Kentish cob-nuts, Whitstable oysters and Dover sole, being a term readily identifiable in the public mind. The cherry was among the first benefits bestowed upon the county by the Romans; and, again, it was the Tudors who made the production of cherries an industry here. We are told that their innovation of building in brick produced the ideal mixture – clay soil and brickdust – for cherry trees to thrive upon. In some small measure, Henry VIII made up to Kent for his ecclesiastical plunderings by importing from France the sweet 'heart cherry', and encouraging the planting of orchards.

Henry Tudor did the county, and therefore all England, another favour by introducing the hop plant from Flanders, and whether by luck or design, fostering its growth in Kentish soil. This is a fairly heavy loam, overlaying pervious subsoils of chalk and gravel, in which hops flourish most happily, encouraged by the necessarily abundant rainfall during the growing period. The 'architecture' of the hop-growing industry is uniquely distinctive: regimented ranks of smartly-strung poles, green garlands entwining them, mellow brick oast houses with their gleaming white-painted wooden cowls, produce together an harmonious blend of the work of nature and of man which even the most rabid abstainer could scarcely begrudge his admiration.

Upon the fourth of Mr Jingle's automatic responses to the mention of Kent, perhaps a male writer would be better equipped to comment. An anonymous one did in a poem, declaring:

> *The maids of Kent! the maids of Kent!*
> *O, language hath no art*
> *To picture to the poet's mind*
> *These idols of the heart!*

Of all the maids of Kent, one more than any bears that title, the so-called Holy Maid. No-one knows much about the origins of Elizabeth

Barton, a humble domestic servant in the sixteenth-century household of Thomas Cobb, whose house at Aldington still stands. At the age of 16 she began to have fits and to fall into trances in which she 'told wondrously things done in other places whilst she was neither herself present'. She also uttered cries of 'marvellous holiness in rebuke of sin and vice', and that was where her undoing began. Thousands flocked to hear her prophecies, which might have remained innocuous enough had she not come to Henry VIII's notice and told him bluntly that if he divorced Queen Katherine to marry Anne Boleyn he would die a villain's death. She was speedily tried for witchcraft and brutally executed. Her advent, though, had had much wider reaching consequences. It had brought to a head the rivalry between Church and State which had festered on over the four centuries since Henry II's henchmen butchered Archbishop Thomas à Becket in Canterbury Cathedral.

The cases of Becket and the Holy Maid are only two of several notable instances of Kent's ability to place thorns beneath the saddle of government. It was a Maidstone man, Wat Tyler, who was the leader of the Peasants' Revolt of 1381, in which London was captured and the boy king Richard II compelled to abolish serfdom. Jack Cade, a Kentish physician and self-styled 'Captain of Kent', headed the insurrection of 1450, marching his ragged army on London to execute justice on Lord Say and Sele, of Knole, who was sheltering in the Tower. And a century later young Sir Thomas Wyatt of Allington led the Kentish men to Southwark in a foolhardy attempt to keep the throne of England from the woman history knows as Bloody Mary.

If the people of Kent have tended to regard themselves as a kingdom in their own right, prepared to go along with the national government so long as the national government will go along with them, this has detracted in no way from their fierce patriotism. As the nearest part of England to the Continent, Kent has borne the brunt of more fighting for British soil than anywhere else. The men in woad fought on the beaches many centuries before that expression was used in Winston Churchill's most defiant speech. The Sea Fencibles of the coastal towns would have been the first line of defence had Bonaparte justified his sneering remark that 'the Channel is a ditch which needs but a pinch of courage to cross'; and in the Second World War it would have been the 'underground army', buried in its ingeniously contrived hides, which would have fought on if the country had been overwhelmed and occupied.

Romans, Saxons, Jutes and Normans, all have had to fight for the privilege of setting foot on Kentish soil. Bonaparte, Kaiser Wilhelm and Adolf Hitler were denied that privilege by Nelson in the Downs, by the Dover Patrol, by the stubborn khaki-clad thousands who sailed to Flanders from Folkestone and returned maimed and exhausted to Dover, by the small craft owners who brought back a later army from Dunkirk, and by the immortal 'Few' who made such Kentish place names as Biggin Hill, Hawkinge and Manston synonymous with those of Hurricane and Spitfire.

Kent's place in what might be termed our island's domestic military history is unique. Every year, her soil yields relics of two thousand years of warfare. Defence works are an ineradicable part of her scenery, from the Roman walls, the Martello Towers and Royal Military Canal, to the 'Hellfire Corner' tablet on Dover's seafront recording no fewer than 464 bombs and 2226 shells rained down on this most battered part of England in the Second World War. And far inland, in the book-lined study of a house dating from Tudor days, there hangs on a wall a diorama of the Mulberry Harbour at Port Arromanches, symbolic of the crowning achievement of one of the greatest of all Englishmen, Winston Churchill, who loved this home of his at Chartwell above all others, and added to it with his own hands as he pondered mighty enterprises or marshalled thoughts and words for another chapter of one of his books. It was at Chartwell that Churchill, pacing his study and dictating to relays of secretaries, wrote some of his most memorable works. Would it be going too far to suggest that Kent herself might have helped to inspire him, as she did another author of high distinction, Elizabeth Bowen, who spent most of her life in the Romney Marsh region and revealed in the fragment of autobiography published after her death in 1973 her debt to Kent, with its dramatic elements of scenery and history which had made her come to regard life as 'a non-stop historical novel . . . disguised only thinly by modern dress'?

Certainly, our greatest dramatist found some inspiration here, using the now-called Shakespeare Cliff at Dover in *King Lear*. And our greatest novelist's works are steeped in the Kent of his boyhood, eager young manhood and broken old age. One has to remind oneself that Charles Dickens wasn't actually born in the county, so closely is he personally identified with it from earliest childhood until his death at Gad's Hill. He had expressly ordered that his bones should remain in Kentish soil for ever – in the moat of Rochester Castle to be precise – but the nation thought otherwise, dishonouring his wish in order to honour his memory in Westminster Abbey.

The only woman occupant of Poets' Corner in the Abbey, incidentally, also came from Kent. She was saucy Aphra Behn, the first professional English authoress, who was born at Wye in 1640. It was a woman, too, who wrote that most considerable verse tribute to the county, the long poem *The Land*: Vita Sackville-West, born at great Knole and creator, with her husband, Harold Nicolson, of the county's principal showplace garden at their home, Sissinghurst Castle. Affection for Kent would be natural enough in writers born here – they include Christopher Smart, Siegfried Sassoon, H. G. Wells, William Hazlitt, Christopher Marlowe, R. S. Barham and Walter de la Mare; but many others who came from elsewhere settled into long residence and sometimes a correspondingly durable love affair with their adopted county. Notable amongst them have been Joseph Conrad, E. Nesbit, H. E. Bates, Richard Church. . . . But one could go on; authors are, and always have been, thick on the ground here in Kent – which, it is worth noticing in passing, produced the man to whom they and all their colleagues owe a debt, William Caxton, the first English printer. The location of his birth is argued over, but it was most likely Tenterden. It was Kent, too, which had the earliest paper mills in England, established before 1590, from which has grown the county's major papermaking industry.

The father of young Wyatt the rebel, Sir Thomas Wyatt the Elder, was also a literary man. He brought the sonnet form to England and is credited with having revived the lyric spirit in English poetry. His castle home at Allington has now become a place of monastic retreat; but it may be visited by the public, as may the birthplace of that other great courtier-poet of his age, Sir Philip Sidney, whose name epitomises Elizabethan courage, grace and chivalry. Penshurst Place, where Queen Elizabeth I once danced on a table top, is one of the many great houses in the county that are preserved and open to view – Knole, Sissinghurst, Ightham Mote and Hever are numbered amongst them. And there is a strength and a beauty in the ancient bricks of such gems as these which is echoed in the solidness and great age of the many smaller weather-boarded or half-timbered houses to be seen in every part of Kent.

There are the castles, too. Proudest and most dramatic of them all is Dover, firmly planted on its hill-top commanding the Channel and ready to shake a mailed fist across it again, should occasion ever arise. Just along the coast are the smaller, clover-leaf-shaped castles built by Henry VIII to defend the shores at Deal and Walmer. The latter is the official residence of the Lord Warden of the Cinque Ports. It was here that the great Duke of Wellington lived his last years; his room, with its simple camp bed and the chair in which he died, is preserved, along with the original Wellington boot. He loved to walk the long straight path before the castle, and on one occasion, pausing in his exercise, he pondered the request of a staff officer that he suggest a token name for the ordinary British soldier, to be printed on specimen forms. Staring out to sea, he recalled the bravery of a dying man in his first command, the 33rd of Foot, who had told him, 'It's all in the day's work, sir'. There, on Walmer beach, the Iron Duke gave his decision and made the name of Thomas Atkins immortal.

Another Kentish castle provides, yet again, a close association with Henry VIII, who seems to have had a potent influence on the county. It is Hever, once home of the Bullen family, and traditionally the place where the course of English history was altered by the chance meeting of Henry with his ill-fated second queen, Anne Boleyn. She is undoubtedly one of Kent's most controversial daughters, denigrated as a scheming virago by some, by others pitied as the hapless plaything of an arrogant and selfish monster.

The bridge at Hever, over which her ghost is said to pass still, spans the River Eden, one of the several less-known rivers of the county which include the delightfully-named Teise, Beult, Swale, Bewl and Wantsum. On a larger, more readily familiar scale, there are also the three Stours (Great, Little and East), the Darent, the eastern Rother and, greatest of all, the Medway, which debouches into the Thames estuary. One effect of some of these waters is to separate parts of the county into the islands which fringe her coastline – Elmley, Grain, Harty, Thanet, Oxney and Sheppey – though in most cases, the 'island' designation is by now merely nominal and one scarcely notices where the mainland ceases and the isles begin.

Kent's relationship with the sea has, in fact, been a two-way one. In places the sea has receded leaving inland townships, such as Sandwich and Richborough, which were once busy ports. Elsewhere it has asserted itself. The infamous Goodwin Sands, for example, were once part of the mainland – but then, millions of years ago, that very land mass had been one with the European continent, with a mere river flowing between, and Kent herself no more than a faceless feature of the whole. Not until the river deepened and widened, engulfing part of the vast plain and separating Britain from the Continent, was this south-eastern corner of the island identified as *cantus*: the rim, or edge, a name which has hardly changed at all through the intervening centuries.

Before this rupture took place, however, the first wave of migrants had arrived in the form of primitive nomadic hunters who appear to have wandered this way in pursuit of plentiful game. It is hard to believe that the lush water meadows where flocks of barrel-bodied, short-legged Romney Marsh sheep now graze were once part of the wild terrain of the rhinoceros, lion, giant deer and bear, animals with whom those Stone Age tribes shared the landscape and whose bones have been discovered amongst those of their hunters in the ancient river gravels of Swanscombe. Remains, too, have been found throughout the county of the temporary camps of later hunters; and at Addington the hearths of a Mesolithic flint industry have been uncovered.

Those impressive shells of great monuments to forgotten gods and kings – I'm thinking particularly of Kits Coty House at Aylesford, Jullieberrie's Grave at Chilham, and the Coldrum Stones at Trottiscliffe – mark a giant step forward in the county's early development, when the nomads' camps were replaced by vigorous young farming communities. The dawn of the age of metal saw the arrival here from the Rhineland area of the Beaker People – so-called from their distinctive flat-bottomed pottery – a sophisticated race which spread rapidly across the eastern and southern parts of the country. And after something like a century and a half of settlement by them and by the Celts, and a subsequent mingling of strains to produce a people we call the Britons, there arrived the Romans, in pursuit of the guerrilla leaders of the Iron Age tribes of Gaul.

Caesar's exploratory visits of 55 and 54 BC in search of these fugitives from across the Channel did not lead to the immediate occupation of the island. That was postponed until the beginning of the Christian era, when the Emperor Claudius initiated what was to be three centuries of Roman rule. But on his latter visit, he gave a foretaste of what was to come by landing in the Deal area – a memorial marks the supposed place – and marching inland to assault Bigberry Camp, the Belgic stronghold close to Canterbury, enforcing at least the nominal submission of the Kentish area.

The Roman occupation of Kent laid the foundations of her future prosperity as England's premier maritime county. The lifeblood of Britannia flowed through the four great ports of *Regulbium* (Reculver), *Rutupiae* (Richborough), *Dubrae* (Dover) and *Portus Lemanis* (Lympne), while the vital artery of Watling Street ran straight from London's south gate, through *Durobrivae* on the Medway, down to *Durovernum Cantiacorum*, chief town of the area and supply depot and inland headquarters of the ports. That occupation has also left indelible marks on the Kent we know today. The ancient capital city of Canterbury covers no-one knows what Roman treasures still waiting to be revealed, Dover has its *pharos*, or lighthouse, and Painted House, and the villa at Lullingstone offers one of the most facinating glimpses of Romano-

British domestic life to be found anywhere.

The legions departed as the Goths swept down on the borders of a crumbling empire, bringing in their wake the obscuring clouds of the Dark Ages. Some of these European *vikingas* made their way across the North Sea; and Kent was one of the first areas to be invaded – though, paradoxically, it was by invitation. Everyone has heard the history of Hengist and Horsa – England's version of Romulus and Remus – but since their story is such a vital part of the county history, it bears re-telling here.

In a fashion true to the traditions of ancient legend, Vortigern, ruler of Kent, in 449 offered part of his kingdom to two brothers of Jutland if they would rid him of marauding Picts. Accordingly, Hengist and Horsa and their warriors sailed in their dragon-prowed ships to Ebbs-fleet on the Isle of Thanet, and speedily despatched the trouble-makers back north where they belonged. They then demanded of Vortigern a far greater area than the Thanet one already agreed on, and in the war which followed won the whole county for themselves at the great and bloody battle of Aylesford. Since Horsa had fallen in the fighting, there was no problem about which of the brothers should be king. Hengist reigned until his death in 488, and was succeeded by his son, Aesc. Incidentally, no-one has finally disproved the belief that the white horse which is Kent's traditional symbol was adopted from the emblem of her Jutish conquerors, who thought so highly of their powerful steeds that they gave their sons such names as Hengist – 'Stallion' – thereby bestowing upon them the gifts of fleetness, strength and majesty. A further belief yet to be disproved is that the Men of Kent are descended from the Jutes, and the Kentish Men from the Saxons; though it has been claimed that the distinction is a purely geographical one, with Men of Kent hailing from the area east of the Medway, and Kentish Men from the west. The rivalry still persists, though only nominally.

The continuous history of the county begins with Hengist's great-great-grandson, Ethelbert, whose marriage to Bertha, Christian daughter of the Frankish king, opened the way for Christianity to enter Kent. The story of Pope Gregory's interest in the blonde and blue-eyed

Anglo-Saxons he encountered in the slave market of Rome is too hackneyed to repeat. What is certain is that in 597 he sent his missionary, St Augustine, with forty other monks, to establish the authority of the Roman see in Britain. So successful were they that Augustine is reported to have baptized in the River Swale no less than 10,000 converts in one day alone, and as a mark of his goodwill, Ethelbert presented the priest with a plot of land on which to build his church – the present site of Canterbury Cathedral. The honour of being the oldest church in continuous use in the county, and indeed the country, is not the cathedral's, however, but neighbouring St Martin's, built by Queen Bertha and her priest some time before St Augustine's arrival, on the foundations of a Christian church of Roman Canterbury. Churches have always been amongst the county's most precious possessions, and rightly so, for Kent is unique in having two entire bishoprics, those of Canterbury and Rochester (the latter created in 604), with many gems of Saxon, Norman and medieval architecture in both dioceses.

The Normans, when they came, proved to be great benefactors to Kent. She was, after all, of vital strategic importance, the strength of England depending – as has often been proved – on the sure defence of this vulnerable corner of the island. Duke William was acting shrewdly when he ignored his new capital until he had assured himself of the fortification of Dover's stronghold, for if Kent were the gateway of England, Dover was the gateway of Kent.

But then, this has always been regarded not only as the first buttress, but as the prime communications link between Britain and the Continent. And communications have played a significant role in the story and the configuration of the county. The coaching roads to Dover and Rochester were the main arteries of trade and travel in both directions, and the railways of Kent were amongst the earliest to be developed, bringing not only commerce to the business centres but profit to the rapidly expanding coastal resorts. The rise of the motor car had its effect too – it is of passing interest that the first motor show ever organised was held in Kent, at Tunbridge Wells in 1895. Flying also has pioneering associations with the county. After all, it was at Dover, in 1909, that Louis Blériot landed after making the first Channel flight of all; and from Lympne some of the trail-blazing flights of the years between the wars commenced.

Now, Kent awaits with a mixture of excitement and trepidation the decision upon its greatest ever communications project, the Channel Tunnel. The county has lived with this promise, or threat, since Napoleonic days, but it has become a stern reality during the past decade or two. To some minds, the 'Chunnel' would bring immense prosperity to Kent, providing much employment, flooding her with far more visitors than the present thrifty day-trippers who come to shop more cheaply than they can in France and Belgium, attracting industry and funnelling tourist traffic. Others see these very things as a dreaded threat to the fair face of the land, envisaging mammoth marshalling yards, monstrous grey warehouses, estates of high-rise flats and all the attendant ugliness that goes with them. At some points in Kent, especially where she meets Essex and London, such sights already exist. But driving through the heart of the Weald on a blue and gold autumn day, it is hard to imagine that it could ever happen here – until one turns a corner, and there, blotting out the landscape, is an industrial monstrosity, a prophetic vision of what could be.

Personally, my priority would be beauty and preservation first. There are, after all, ample ways of getting between the Continent and Kent – some people even do it by swimming. Once more I echo the sentiments expressed by Michael Drayton in *Polyolbion*:

> *O noble Kent . . .*
> *The hard'st to be controlled, impatientest of wrong . . .*
> *Of all the English shires be thou surnamed the Free,*
> *And foremost ever placed, when they shall reckoned be . . .*

Royal Tunbridge Wells, 1976

WICKHAMBREUX

Historic, peaceful and picturesque, the village of Wickhambreux, a few miles east of Canterbury, is justly considered to be one of the beauty spots of East Kent. It stands on the banks of the Little Stour, whose waters once powered the great paddle wheel of the weather-boarded mill pictured here. The mill is mechanised now, and the wheel within its slatted covering turns only to delight the visitor.

Round to the left and over the bridge is the pretty village green with Georgian houses of individual character spaced around it beneath the limes and chestnuts. More lime-trees line the avenue to the medieval church, which has – somewhat surprisingly – a unique Art Nouveau stained glass window. The post office is housed in an ancient building with chequered walls of flint and stone, a nice contrast to the timbering and brickwork about. Antiques are sold at one shop, cream teas at another, and the Wooden Horse inn provides entertainment as a centre for morris dancers, whose grotesque horse-mask is depicted on the sign.

The village name (pronounced Wickhambroo) derives its affix from the thirteenth-century family of de Brewse, or de Braiose, to whom the original estate here belonged.

IGHTHAM MOTE

Whose Arte disclosd that Plot, which had it taken,
Rome had tryumph'd & Britans walls had shaken . . .

So runs the final couplet of an epitaph in Ightham church on the monument to Dame Dorothy Selby, who may, or may not – historians are still undecided – have been responsible for the anonymous warning which saved King and Parliament from Guy Fawkes's Gunpowder Plot in 1605.

For three centuries, until the 1880s, the Selby family were the owners of Ightham Mote, a lovely medieval manor house close to the hamlet of Ivy Hatch by Ightham village. Set within its moat, fed by the Shode stream, the house dates from the early fourteenth century, with extensive rebuilding in Tudor times adding timbered upper storeys and the imposing gatehouse.

The earliest known owner was Sir Thomas Cawne, at the end of the fourteenth century, but an earlier one planned the Great Hall, seen here on the right of the courtyard. This was build *c.* 1340, though the window belongs to the following century. The Solar Wing, at left, with twin gables and timbered oriel window, is Tudor.

In private ownership still, Ightham Mote is open to the public on Friday afternoons.

LEEDS CASTLE

Standing on its twin islands in the River Len, Leeds Castle rises romantically above the reed-fringed waters of its moat-lake. It is privately owned, but extensive views may be had from the A20 road south of Hollingbourne, skirting 'Capability' Brown's landscaped grounds.

The earliest part of the castle dates from the beginning of the twelfth century, when Robert de Crevecoeur erected a motte-and-bailey defence on the site, but only the cellars survive of this building. It later passed into the possession of the Crown, the walls and turrets being constructed during the reign of Edward I, whose favourite residence this was. Some damage resulted to the fabric when the castle was successfully beseiged in 1321, after Bartholomew de Badlesmere, who held the place for Edward II, had joined the Lancastrian party against the effeminate king. Additional building carried out during the first half of the sixteenth century included the Maiden's Tower, and the Gloriette, or arbour, which is reached by a two-storey stone bridge joining the two islands.

In 1632 the property was bought by Sir Thomas Colepeper. His descendant, Fiennes Wykeham-Martin, inherited in 1821 and largely constructed the main buildings, giving Leeds Castle its present battlemented appearance.

CANTERBURY: THE WESTGATE

To the Iron Age Britons it was *Durovernon*: fastness in the swamps; and to the Saxons, *Cantwara burh*: stronghold of the Kentish men. Kent's greatest cathedral city, founded on as great a Roman town, Canterbury dominates the county's history.

Here, at Westgate, was the Roman London Gate, where roads from Dover, Lympne and Richborough met at the junction of Watling Street, artery to a young capital. The original gate was part of the city wall, enclosing an area of 120 acres, erected in the third century AD – the size and compactness of the settlement is reflected in that of modern Canterbury 'town'. Westgate is the sole survivor of the seven gates which gave access to the medieval walled city, and in its present form dates from the late fourteenth century. It was used for some time as the city prison, and the cells may still be seen in the room above the gateway. From the battlements there is a fine view of the western end of the cathedral, rising above a clutter of red-tiled roofs.

Close to Westgate is the Falstaff Hotel, a fifteenth-century hostelry whose antiquity is shared by neighbouring rows of high, half-timbered houses.

FAIRFIELD CHURCH IN ROMNEY MARSH

Until a causeway was built across the fields here, Fairfield church stood isolated on its small island in Romney Marsh. In wet weather, when the surrounding land was flooded, parishioners arrived by boat.

The thirteenth-century church is one of the wonders of the Marsh. It was meant to serve as a temporary structure only, but has survived the intervening centuries, and in 1913 was encased in brick to preserve the original timbers. It is the only church dedicated to St Thomas à Becket in the diocese of Canterbury.

This part of Kent is a unique peninsula covered by the marshes of Romney, Denge and Walland, and is bordered to the north by the Royal Military Canal, built during the Napoleonic wars to defend the country between Hythe and the Rother, just over the Sussex border. The rich, fertile plain of dyke-divided water meadows where thousands of Romney sheep now feed once lay beneath the sea, but reclamation began as early as Roman times, when the Rhee Wall was established. Because of the isolation and emptiness of the area, it was formerly a haunt of smugglers, who hid their contraband lace, brandy and tobacco in the small churches and lonely marshland farms.

BROADSTAIRS HARBOUR

What William Shakespeare is to Stratford-upon-Avon, Charles Dickens is to Broadstairs. He spent many summer holidays here with his family between 1837 and 1851, first at Albion Street and Lawn House, and latterly at Fort House, which – now renamed Bleak House – presides over the small harbour.

He worked here on several major novels, including *Nicholas Nickleby, The Old Curiosity Shop,* and the autobiographical *David Copperfield*; but not, ironically, *Bleak House*: this he wrote after the noise of German bands and other street musicians had driven him away from Broadstairs in search of peace and quiet elsewhere. An annual Dickens Festival has been held in the town since 1937 and Bleak House has been partly turned into a museum of Dickensiana.

Where a cornfield stood in his time, between the house and the beach, there is now a comfortable huddle of roofs and mellow-toned walls fringing Viking Bay. Close to the weatherboarded Harbour Master's office on the mole protecting the bay stands the Tartar Frigate inn, seen here below Bleak House. Since the days of Victoria it has been a favourite port of call for the many sailors and fishermen whose craft ply in and out of the harbour.

KNOLE

One of the finest stately houses of England is Knole, home of the Sackvilles, dukes of Dorset, since the beginning of the seventeenth century. It stands on its hillslope like a medieval walled town, encircled by the great trees of its deer park.

The present building dates from the 1460s, when Thomas Bourchier, Archbishop of Canterbury, acquired the manor of Knole, at Sevenoaks, and set about turning the old manor house into a splendid palace. It remained the property of successive primates until Cranmer prudently made a gift of it to Henry VIII. In 1566 it was leased from Queen Elizabeth by her cousin, Sir Thomas Sackville, who liked the place so well that he bought it from the Crown in 1603. The interior of the house owes much to the remodelling which Sir Thomas carried out, his main purpose being to create a series of sumptuously decorated state rooms in the south range of the old palace. The Great Staircase, seen here, typifies the ornate Jacobean character of his work – though the reclining form of Giannetta Baccelli, mistress of the 3rd Duke of Dorset, is a later attraction.

Now National Trust property, Knole remains the family home of the Sackvilles.

BLOSSOM AND OAST HOUSES AT GOLDEN GREEN

There is no scene more evocative of rural Kent than fruit blossom and oast houses, such as those pictured here at the village of Golden Green, near Hadlow.

The distinctive circular oasts were introduced into the county in the early 1800s, replacing the more usual square kilns which had been used to dry the hops since the plant had first been brought to England from Flanders in the sixteenth century.

Planting commences with the first spell of fine weather in late January or early February, and the hop gardens – as the fields are known – are networked with the familiar pattern of fibre string, supported by wires attached to stout poles, along which the growing hops, or bines, entwine themselves. Harvesting begins at the end of August, and until recent years marked the annual summer exodus of many thousands of Londoners, when the entire East End descended on the Kentish countryside for hop-picking.

Half the hops in the country are grown here; and the apple, pear and cherry orchards make this 'Garden of England' the most important fruit-producing county in Britain. The national Apple and Pear Development Council is based at Tunbridge Wells.

MAIDSTONE: THE ARCHBISHOP'S PALACE

One of Maidstone's most attractive features is its medieval Archbishop's Palace, whose walls are reflected in the waters of the River Medway. It was built in the mid-fourteenth century with stone taken from an older building at Wrotham, some miles away, and served as a palace for the archbishops of Canterbury until the Reformation. There was some rebuilding in Tudor times, resulting in the finely proportioned front.

The Palace's great Tithe Barn is close by in Mill Street and now houses the fine Tyrwhitt-Drake coach collection.

Upriver from the Palace is All Saints Church, the parish church of Maidstone. Dating from the end of the fourteenth century, it has been described as the grandest Perpendicular church in Kent. Many of the stalls in the chancel have carved misericords, one showing the figure of a man brandishing ladle and meat-hook: this is thought to represent the cook at Archbishop Courtenay's College nearby, which the church was built to serve.

Although Maidstone was not incorporated until 1549, its central position favoured its pre-eminence as county town of Kent over Canterbury, the old 'capital'. It still retains much of the busy atmosphere of a market town.

TENTERDEN

Tile-hung, weatherboarded, red-bricked or half-timbered, the houses in Tenterden's high street reflect the building fashions of successive generations, from early Tudor to late Georgian. Lining one side of the wide thoroughfare at the heart of this small Wealden town, they look across to neat grass borders and cottage gardens of hollyhock, lupin and rose.

Tenterden was originally *Tenetwara denn*: the woodland pasture of the men of Thanet, the land here being the property of the Saxon manor of Minster-in-Thanet. A further reminder of the connection is the dedication of the town's thirteenth-century church to St Mildred, abbess of Minster. The handsome church tower of grey Bethersden marble was given by the local community of Flemish weavers in 1461, at a time when Tenterden was an important centre of the broadcloth industry. Its goods were carried from the port of Smallhythe close by, and as a corporate member of the Cinque Ports it remained one of the most prosperous of the Wealden towns until its harbour on the Rother estuary became stranded inland as the river silted up.

Tenterden remains a thriving little town, though, and is the main shopping centre for the many pretty villages roundabout.

THE ROMNEY, HYTHE & DYMCHURCH RAILWAY

The longest steam-operated line remaining in the country, and the longest 15″ gauge railway in the world, is the Romney, Hythe & Dymchurch Light Railway, which has been running a regular service between these Romney Marsh towns since 1926.

In that year the main section of the track was opened to link up the Southern Rail terminals at Hythe and New Romney, followed three years later by the extension to Dungeness. The line now boasts a track of almost 23 miles, carrying 70 coaches drawn by replicas of famous steam locomotives of the past. Although the engines, such as no. 10, *Doctor Syn*, seen here, are scaled-down versions, only one-third the size of the originals, they are anything but toys, and can travel at speeds of 20 m.p.h. hauling comfortable old-style carriages full of shoppers and tourists. For enthusiasts, there is a 'model railway land' at the New Romney terminal.

Kent's other steam railway is the partly-reopened Kent & East Sussex, running between Headcorn and Robertsbridge. It was built in 1900 for the use of farmers in the area, and called at Tenterden and at Rolvenden, where the station now houses a museum and a superb collection of steam engines and rolling stock.

CANTERBURY CATHEDRAL

Cradle of English Christendom and seat of the Primate of All England, shrine to the memory of the 'hooly blisful martir', St Thomas à Becket, the Cathedral Church of Christ at Canterbury has a spiritual history spanning fourteen centuries.

It commenced in 597 with the Christian missionary, St Augustine, to whom the site was granted by Ethelbert of Kent on which to build his church. A Saxon cathedral followed, to be considerably enlarged by Lanfranc after his consecration as first Norman archbishop in 1070. The foundations of this substantial church stand beneath the great cathedral begun by his successor, Anselm, at the beginning of the twelfth century. Subsequent rebuilding resulted in the magnificent choir, nave and transepts which are among the cathedral's most striking features. The first major restoration was carried out between 1820–48, and more repair work was necessary after the Second World War, though fortunately the fabric escaped serious bomb damage.

For almost four hundred years, until the Reformation, the focal point of pilgrimage was the crypt, in which was entombed the body of St Thomas à Becket after his murder here in 1170. The character of the countless pilgrims who journeyed to pray at the shrine has been immortalised by Chaucer in his *Canterbury Tales*.

SCOTNEY CASTLE

Old Scotney, near Lamberhurst, owes its romantically decayed appearance to the nineteenth-century passion for picturesque scenery, and was intentionally ruined to form the centrepiece of the view from new Scotney Castle, on the hill behind.

The oldest part of the ruins is one of the four circular corner towers – its battlements now replaced by a conical roof and lantern – belonging to a small moated castle built on a tributary of the River Teise towards the end of the fourteenth century. The living quarters, rebuilt during the sixteenth century, were considerably enlarged a little over a hundred years later to complete the transformation from castle to country mansion. When Edward Hussey had new Scotney Castle built in 1837, the already neglected buildings were further damaged in order to create an idyllic view of the valley, with the creeper-clad ruins reflected in the waters of the moat. Stone for the new house was taken from the hillside, leaving a quarry which was carefully framed with forest trees and planted with flowering shrubs, resulting in the beautiful gardens here today.

Old Scotney and its grounds were bequeathed to the National Trust by Edward Hussey's grandson, the writer Christopher Hussey, on his death in 1970.

MEOPHAM

Cricket on the green at Meopham, played against the background of the appropriately named pub, The Cricketers, which stands beside one of the finest smock mills in the south of England: the scene is a cameo of the best of rural Kent, a county proud of its many lovely villages, its old and welcoming inns offering as good beer and food as any in the country, its enduring relics of cottage industries, and, not least of all, of its cricketing history.

Some of the earliest matches recorded were played in Kent, or by Kentish teams 'away'. The county club, formed in 1859, has its headquarters at Canterbury, and 'Canterbury Week', held at the beginning of August, is one of the most exciting highlights of the season. Few England teams have not included one or more Kent players, some of whose names live in the game's history and legend: 'the Lion of Kent', Alfred Mynn; Frank Woolley, one of the most graceful and prolific batsmen of all time; Colin Cowdrey, the world's top scorer of Test runs; Percy Chapman, brilliant fielder and dashing captain; and that line of exceptional wicket-keepers, Leslie Ames, Godfrey Evans and Alan Knott.

ROCHESTER: THE CORN EXCHANGE

The Corn Exchange building was presented to Rochester by its M.P., Rear-Admiral Sir Cloudesley Shovel, in 1706, a year before he was drowned when his flag-ship foundered off the Scilly Isles. Its enormous clock projects above the High Street, looking 'as if Time carried on business and hung out his sign' in the opinion of Charles Dickens, who made the city the Cloisterham in which his last, unfinished novel, *The Mystery of Edwin Drood* is set.

Rochester stands on the site of Roman *Durobrivae*: stronghold at the bridges, guarding a vital crossing on the Medway of Watling Street, running from London to Dover. The castle, dominating the city, was built on older foundations in 1087, its keep – the highest in the country – being added half a century later. A previous stronghold here is referred to in a charter of 670, in which the prelate of Rochester is named as 'Bishop of the Castle of West Kent'.

Rochester is the second oldest see in England, its first bishop being Justus, a companion of St Augustine from Rome, ordained in 604. The Norman cathedral, as well as the castle, is the work of the architect of the White Tower of London, Bishop Gundulf.

RAMSGATE HARBOUR

In the days of the first Elizabeth, Ramsgate was a tiny fishing village of no more than twenty-five dwellings perched at the south-eastern corner of the Isle of Thanet. It remained a secluded backwater until the late eighteenth century, when its bracing air and proximity to London gained it popularity as a coastal resort, while sea trade with the Continent turned the quiet harbour into an increasingly busy port.

Regency influence is still noticeable in the town's character: elegant houses line the approaches and low summits of the East and West Cliffs; street names such as The Plains of Waterloo and La Belle Alliance Square proclaim patriotic pleasure at Bonaparte's defeat; and beside the harbour rears the obelisk (seen at extreme right) raised to mark George IV's departure from Ramsgate to visit Hanover in 1822. On his return he repaid the compliment by bestowing the title of 'Royal Harbour' on the town.

The harbour, with its enclosing piers, consists of two basins, the outer one for commercial shipping, the other a marina for pleasure craft. Pegwell Bay, now virtually an extension of Ramsgate, lies to the south-west and is the main hoverport for cross-Channel traffic.

HEVER CASTLE

One of the most dramatic love stories of all time began at Hever on a spring day in 1522 when, tradition says, Henry VIII first saw Anne Boleyn as she walked in the grounds among the early flowers. During the long and stormy courtship which followed, she frequently returned in search of the solitude denied her at Court; and her sad ghost is to be seen here still, crossing the bridge each Christmastide.

Anne's grandfather, Sir William Bullen, was responsible for much of the rebuilding of this late fourteenth-century manor house, which stands within a moat-lake formed by the River Eden. He had inherited from his father, Sir Geoffrey, who purchased Hever in 1462. Three generations later the castle was confiscated by King Henry and presented to his more fortunate fourth wife, Anne of Cleves, but it was little used and fell into decay, becoming a lowly farmhouse for a time.

In 1903 Hever was bought by the American millionaire, William Waldorf Astor, who had the building completely restored to its former Tudor splendour. The castle is still privately owned by the Astor family and, together with the attractive gardens, is open to the public for part of the year.

TUNBRIDGE WELLS: THE PANTILES

Princes and poets, gamblers and gourmands alike came to drink the waters of the Wells at Tunbridge during its days as a fashionable spa resort.

The chalybeate spring here had been discovered by Lord North in 1606, and the spot quickly became a popular summer venue. Lack of accommodation obliged Queen Henrietta Maria to camp on the Common when she visited in 1630, but a generation later lodging houses were doing brisk business on the slopes of Mount Sion and Mount Ephraim, and by the end of the century a sizeable village had grown up.

The original lane of stalls and refreshment booths leading to the Wells had developed by the mid-eighteenth century into the gracious colonnaded parade known as The Pantiles, taking its name from the large roofing tiles used to pave it, and in the spa's heyday fashionable society met here to gossip and gamble and to relieve 'cold chronical distempers, weak nerves and bad digestion'.

During the nineteenth century the town's image shifted as the age of the rake and roué gave way to that of Victorian respectability; but Tunbridge Wells remains, though for different reasons now, one of Kent's most attractively popular resorts.

BARFRESTON CHURCH

Apart from the great cathedrals of Canterbury and Rochester, the finest example of Norman craftsmanship in Kent is the church of St Nicholas, at Barfreston. It was built a little before 1180 in the Romanesque style which marked the early medieval renaissance in the county, and, apart from some necessary rebuilding in the mid-nineteenth century, has mercifully escaped 'restoration', with no tower or turret added to mar the strength and simplicity of the original design.

The interior – hardly more than 15 metres long – is dominated by its high chancel arch, beyond which is a great wheel-shaped window set into the gable end, each of its eight spokes, or colonnettes, banded by winged beasts emerging from leaf-shapes.

What makes Barfreston church such a splendid inheritance is the wealth of stone carving bequeathed by those unknown craftsmen, such as the grotesque heads lining the gables of the outer walls. But the masterpiece is the detailed decoration above the south doorway, pictured here, where sunken medallions depicting labours of the months, zodiac signs and animal fantasies which only the medieval mind could conceive, arch in bands above a seated Christ, surrounded by angel forms and mythical beasts.

CHARTWELL

'Every day away from Chartwell is a day wasted', said Sir Winston Churchill of his home near Westerham in the Kentish Weald. He bought the pleasant Tudor manor house in 1922, and it remained the favourite family home until his death in 1965.

The house – now National Trust property – still contains many mementoes of the great statesman: his paintings line the walls, his hats and walking sticks lend a casual air, and in what is now the Museum Room is displayed the famous Boer War poster offering a reward for the young Churchill's capture *levend of dood*: living or dead.

The most personal room is the study, pictured here, dominated by a replica of Sir Winston's Garter Banner. Over the fireplace hangs a study of his birthplace, Blenheim Palace, and his desk is cluttered with family photographs. It was here that he worked during the years of political wilderness in the 1930s, writing his life of Marlborough, and, later, his chronicle of the Second World War and the *History of the English-speaking Peoples*.

The grounds of Chartwell are an added attraction and enclose Churchill's cottage studio and the wall which he built himself around the kitchen garden.

PENSHURST PLACE

Elizabethan England's most 'parfit gentil knight', the poet, soldier and diplomat, Sir Philip Sidney, was born at Penshurst Place, near Tunbridge, in 1554. He died in the Netherlands, aged only 32, but his spirit, and his love for his birthplace, endure in the lines of *Arcadia*, which has its setting here and in the surrounding Kentish countryside.

Penshurst has been in the possession of the Sidney family since 1552, when Edward VI granted it to his Chamberlain and Steward of the Household, Sir William Sidney. Its first owner was Sir John de Pulteney, a merchant of London and four times Lord Mayor, who built his country house here in the 1340s. Of this original building the great hall still stands, at the right in this view of the south front of Penshurst Place. The Buckingham Buildings at centre, and the Elizabethan galleries forming the western flank of the forecourt, are later additions to the house.

Penshurst village close by is of interest in its own right, with a square and Victorian cottages in a medieval style which blends happily with Penshurst Place. The present owner, Viscount De L'Isle, opens the house and its notable gardens to the public for much of the year.

DOVER: THE CASTLE AND WEST DOCK

The history of Dover can be said to epitomise that of England, for it may be traced from the Iron Age to the European Economic Community. Julius Caesar was prevented from landing here; William the Conqueror made sure of the town's defences before claiming England; and servicemen of two world wars sailed home past its White Cliffs.

Dover Castle, high above the harbour, stands on ground which has been fortified since the Iron Age, when massive ramparts enclosed the top of the East Cliff. The Romans erected a *pharos*, or lighthouse, here to act as a beacon for galleys crossing from Gaul, and the Saxons built the Church of St Mary-in-Castro (seen at right) beneath its sturdy walls. The Conqueror reinforced the defences with a timber palisade; but it was Henry II who, in 1168, began work on the great castle. It was garrisoned by 1185, and was to remain so until 1958.

Dover's first harbour was enclosed at the end of the fifteenth century, and was called 'Pleasant' by gratified mariners. Their little harbour now lies beneath the western dock area pictured here, part of the port which, as Britain's gateway to Europe, is busy the entire year round.

BIDDENDEN

Biddenden's charming village sign depicts its most famous residents, the siamese twins who are affectionately referred to as 'The Maids'. Eliza and Mary Chulkhurst were born here in West Kent, so tradition says, about the year 1100, and remained joined at hip and shoulder until their deaths at the age of 34, conveniently expiring within a few hours of each other. They are locally remembered each Easter by the distribution of decorated biscuits, a custom perpetuating the old belief that The Maids were the founders of an annual charity which provided quartern loaves and cheese for the poor of the parish.

The village's outstanding attraction, though, is the Old Cloth Hall (seen at left), a long half-timbered building with a splendid tile-hung roof, standing at one end of the main street. It was built in the sixteenth century as a centre for the cloth industry in this area and was originally the home of the master-clothier, though it was later extended to serve as a manufactory, containing several weavers' workshops.

The thirteenth-century church of All Saints at the further end of the street possesses some fine brass memorials to prosperous Tudor cloth merchants and their families.

SISSINGHURST CASTLE

'I fell in love; love at first sight. I saw what might be made of it. It was Sleeping Beauty's Castle: but a castle running away into sordidness and squalor; a garden crying out for rescue.' This is how the author and poet Vita Sackville-West described her first impression of Sissinghurst Castle, near Cranbrook. She and her diplomat husband, Harold Nicolson, bought it in 1930 and devoted the next ten years to restoring the ruined buildings and creating, from a wilderness, the gardens which are now a national showplace.

The Elizabethan manor house was built by Sir Richard Baker on the site of an earlier house, of which only the entrance range remains. The four-storeyed gate tower, pictured here, would have been a recent addition when Queen Elizabeth visited Sissinghurst in 1573.

The fortunes of the house declined, though, and in the 1750s it became a prison for French seamen, whose term for it, 'chateau', led to it being called a castle. The resulting damage to the fabric was such that the main buildings were demolished about 1800, and what remained was used as a rubbish dump until rescued by the Nicolsons. Sissinghurst Castle is now National Trust property.